Anonymous

# Litanies for the Choirs in the Congregations of the United Brethren

Anonymous

**Litanies for the Choirs in the Congregations of the United Brethren**

ISBN/EAN: 9783337296643

Printed in Europe, USA, Canada, Australia, Japan

Cover: Foto ©Thomas Meinert / pixelio.de

More available books at **www.hansebooks.com**

# LITANIES

FOR THE

CHOIRS IN THE CONGREGATIONS

OF THE

*UNITED BRETHREN,*

REVISED AND ENLARGED.

---

LONDON:

PRINTED IN THE YEAR 1793.

A Revised and enlarged edition of the general Liturgy-Book for the Congregations of the United Brethren having been publiſhed; our next endeavor has been, to ſatisfy the deſire of our Congregations, by publiſhing likewiſe a new edition of Litanies for the reſpective Choirs. It conſiſts of the following Litanies:

I. For the Children;

II. For the Single Brethren;

III. For the Single Siſters;

IV. For the Married Brethren and Siſters;

V. For the Widowers; and,

VI. For the Widows.

Theſe are now delivered to the ſaid Choirs, with a renewed cordial wiſh, that

our

our dear Lord and Savior may richly impart unto each of theſe diviſions of his Congregation, from the fulneſs of his holy merits, all that is requiſite for their ſtate and calling; and that unto Him the Holy Ghoſt may perfect new praiſes out of their hearts and mouths.

Thus unto JESUS JEHOVAH
All Choirs will render praiſes,
When each to him Hallelujah,
With—Lord have mercy!—raiſes.

# I.

# LITANIES OF THE CHILDREN.

## 1*.

*L.* LORD GOD OUR FATHER, WHICH ART IN HEAVEN!

*A. Hallowed be thy name; thy kingdom come; thy will be done on earth, as it is in Heaven; give us this day our daily bread; and forgive us our treſpaſſes, as we forgive them that treſpaſs againſt us; and lead us not into temptation, but deliver us from evil;*

*L.* For thine is the kingdom and the power and the glory, for ever and ever,

*A. Amen!*

T. 22. b.

1. Thee, Abba, Father! we revere
For calling us thy children dear;
*G.* A father's heart we find in thee,
*B.* Since Chriſt our Brother deign'd to be.

*A.* 2. Thou haſt the world ſo greatly lov'd,
That thou, by boundleſs mercy mov'd,
Didſt give thy well-beloved Son,
By death for all our ſins t' atone;

* *A.* is ſung by *all* the children; *B.* by the boys; *L.* by the liturgiſt; and *G.* by the girls.

*B.* 3. That he all, who in him believe,
Might in thy family receive.
*A.* May we this living faith obtain,
And faithful to the end remain.

*L.* LORD GOD HOLY GHOST!
*A.* *Abide with us for ever!*

T. 22. o.

*B.* 4. God Holy Spirit! thee we praiſe
For thy inſtructions, gifts, and grace,
*G.* And for declaring unto us
Our Savior's ſuff'rings, wounds, and croſs.

*A.* 5. Grant, that we all attentive be,
And prove obedient unto thee
For all the grace thou doſt afford
In leading us to Chriſt our Lord.

*G.* 6. O let our needy ſouls by faith
Enjoy the merits of Chriſt's death!
*B.* And may his precious blood bedew,
And hallow all we think or do.

*L.* LORD GOD SON, THOU SAVIOR OF THE WORLD!
*A.* *Own us to be thine!*

T. 22. d.

7. Jeſus, the children's deareſt friend,
*G.* Who doſt to all our wants attend,
*A.* Thou waſt a child, and knoweſt well
How we, thy helpleſs children, feel.

*B.* 8. We humbly thee approach, and greet
With reverence thy pierced ſeet;
*G.* We kiſs thy hand, which hath beſtow'd
On us, thy children, ſo much good.

T. 22. c.

*A.* 9. Embrace us in thy tender way,
And bleſs us all, we humbly pray,
As thou on earth didſt formerly,
When they young children brought to thee.

10. We are baptiz'd into thy death,
And call'd to praiſe thee with each breath;
Thou'ſt bought us with thy blood divine,
O take and keep us ever thine!

T. 4. 2d p.

*L.* Our children ſhall be
Both now and for ever devoted to thee.

T. 235.

*A.* 11. *The grace of our Lord Jeſus Chriſt,*
*The love of God, ſo highly priz'd,*
*The Holy Ghoſt's communion be*
*With all of us moſt ſenſibly.*
*Amen!*

## 2.

*L.* OUR LORD CHRIST JESUS,
*A.* *Be gracious unto us!*

T. 132. a. 2d p.

*Sung.* Thou ſlaughter'd Lamb, our God and Lord,
To needy pray'rs thine ear afford,
And on us all have mercy!

*L.* From all coldneſs to thy merits and death,
From all ſelf-complacency,
From levity and ſelf-will,
From all hypocriſy and diſſimulation,
From all ſeduction,
From the wiles and devices of Satan,
From a worldly and carnal mind,
From all ſin,
*A.* *Preſerve us, our dear Lord and God!*

T. 132. a.

*L.* Lord Jeſus, to thy grace divine,
Thy faithful care and favor,
Theſe children we commend: They're thine,
And ſhall be thine for ever.

O may each in thy nail-prints ſee
Its grace-election, and in thee
Be found at thy appearing.

T. 206.

*B.* My king benign,
*G.* My king benign,
*A.* We'd fain be thine;

Not any thing,
G. No ſmall
A. No ſmalleſt hankering
Cauſe us, while here we ſtay,
Moſt faithful Lord, from thee to ſtray;
No, may each breath—exalt thy death,
And ſing thy praiſe,
G. And ſing thy praiſe
For thy unbounded grace,
A. For thy unbounded grace!

L. With all the merits of thy life,
A. *Bleſs us, our dear Lord and God!*

L. By thy holy incarnation and birth,
A. Make our human nature dear to us!

T. 22. b.

*Sung.* Welcome, O welcome Lamb of God,
Who haſt aſſum'd our fleſh and blood,
Since thou for us haſt liv'd and died,
Our human nature 's ſanctified.

L. By thy holy childhood
A. Make us partakers of child-like joy!
L. By thy obedience and ſubjection
A. Grant unto us obedient hearts!
L. Thy blameleſs walk on earth,
A. Be our comfort and example!

T. 22. d.

*Sung.* Thy youth unſpotted, full of grace,
Teach us all virtue and all praiſe,
Thou art our pattern, grant that we
In all things may reſemble thee!

L. With thine agony and bloody ſweat,
With thy being bound, buffeted, and reviled,

With thy being ſcourged and crowned with thorns,
With thy ignominious crucifixion,
With thy holy wounds,
With thy precious blood,
With thy meritorious death,
With thy reſurrection and aſcenſion,
*A.* *Bleſs us, our dear Lord and God!*

T. 79. 2d p.

*Sung.* O may we for thy paſſion
And death for our ſalvation,
Be as thy trophies ſoon diſplayed!

*L.* With thy coming again to thy church, or our being call'd home to thee,
*A.* *Comfort us, our dear Lord and God!*

T. 132. a.

*Sung.* His goodneſs and his mercies all
Will follow us for ever,
And we'll maintain our proper call,
To cleave to our dear Savior,
And to his Congregation here,
And when call'd home, we ſhall live there,
With Chriſt, our ſoul's Redeemer.

T. 539. a.

*L.* Chriſt, thou Lamb of God, which takeſt away the ſins of the world,
Leave thy peace with them!
*A.* Amen.

## 3.

T. 519.

*A.* MOST holy Lord and God,
*B.* Holy almighty God,
*G.* Holy and moſt merciful Savior,
*A.* Thou eternal God!
Lamb of God unſpotted,
To our pray'rs O lend an ear,
Have mercy, O Lord!

T. 235.

Here are we children poor and mean,
O make us thine and waſh us clean,
Grant, that both ſoul and body may
Thy merits ſhare from day to day!
Till we ſhall with the Church above
Unite to praiſe redeeming love:
Amen.

T. 22. b.

*B.* 1. Thy bleſt humanity on earth
Shows us our human nature's worth;
*G.* Grant, that thy childhood may impart
True child-like joy to ev'ry heart.

*B.* 2. From year to year—whilſt we increaſe
In ſtature—may we grow in grace,
*G.* In learning and obedience too
May we thy bleſſed path purſue.

T. 22. d.

*B.* 3. Thy bloody ſweat and agony
Fill us with fervent love to thee,

*G.* Thy thorny crown, thy crofs and pain
Our glory, joy, and ftrength remain.

*A.* 4. Yea, with thy death, O Lamb of God,
With thy bleft wounds and precious blood,
With all thy fuff'rings and diftrefs,
Us, thy poor Children, ever blefs.

T. 22. e.

5. Thus will our infant tongues record
The death and fuff'rings of our Lord,
That thou, who diedft in our ftead,
Art God, by whom all things were made.

6. Thee, gracious Lord, we now implore,
To manifeft thyfelf ftill more,
And thus to teach us by degrees,
To live a life of happinefs.

*G.* 7. May we thy mind ftill better know,
*B.* May we in grace and knowledge grow,
*A.* And learn all that, whereby we may
Adorn thy doctrine ev'ry way.

T. 22. l.

8. By day and night our fteps direct,
And foul and body, Lord, protect
From ev'ry thing, that grieveth thee,
Or unto us might hurtful be.

9. Impart to us each needful good,
A heart, befprinkled with thy blood,
Thankful and wholly giv'n to thee
For thy foul's bitter agony.

T. 235.

O may we ever feel thee near,
And be employ'd in praife and pray'r,

In

In feeble accents we'll proclaim
The glories of thy ſaving name.
Amen.

4. T. 9.

*L.* CHRIST our Savior look on thee,
Children's congregation!
Thou art his, becauſe that he
Purchas'd thy ſalvation.

*A.* Thine we are, thine we'll remain,
Jeſus, till in glory
We, when our faith's end we gain,
Seeing ſhall adore thee.

*L.* May we not his grace enjoy
Here on earth already?
What effect is wrought thereby
Both in ſoul and body?

*A.* Quite unutterable is
What our hearts are feeling
Of divine delight and bliſs
At his kind revealing.

We with deep humility
Give him thanks and praiſes;
But who can ſufficiently
Laud him for his mercies?

T. 14. a.

*L.* While in this vale of tears ye dwell,
What is your greateſt bliſs?

*A.* When Jeſu's precious peace we feel,
And when we're own'd as his.

*L.* What is your higheſt wiſh and aim?
*A.* To live unto his praiſe,
His love and goodneſs to proclaim,
And pleaſe him all our days.

T. 1.

*L.* May he theſe choiceſt bleſſings on you ſhow'r
For all his ſuff'rings ſake, for evermore.

*A.* Bleſs us poor children with thy precious blood,
O'erſtream us ſinners with that cleanſing flood.

*L.* What will you render to him on your part?
*A.* We nothing have to give but our poor heart.

T. 58. 2d p.

Truſting in his mercy we will adore him,
And humbly walk in grace and truth before him,
Till we go hence.

T. 119.

*L.* For his death,
*G.* For his death,
*A.* He is worthy evermore,
That the children's congregation
His moſt precious name adore,
And extol his great ſalvation,
Yea, that all in earth and heaven bow
'Fore him low.

T. 22. e.

*L.* Devote yourſelves to him anew
As his reward and purchaſe due;

Thus will his bleſſing you attend,
Until in him your race ſhall end.

T. 36.

*A.* Grant, that we all may bloom for thee like flowers
Unto thy praiſe, thro' thy atonement's powers,
Yea, magnify thy name in us for ever,
Moſt gracious Savior!

# II.

## LITANIES OF THE SINGLE BRETHREN.

### 1*.

T. 235.

*A.* FATHER of all things thou,
And Mediator too,
Jehovah Sabaoth,
Life, who once tasted death!
*Ch.* Angels and men thy lauds proclaim,
And magnify thy saving name.
*A.* In Heav'n and earth one voice doth sound:
Thou hast by death for us aton'd!
Upholder of all things confest,
Remain thou on our hearts impress'd,
As in our flesh and blood array'd,
In all things like thy brethren made,
Yet without sin, thou didst thereby
Our human nature sanctify;
May we for this thy boundless grace
In soul and body give thee praise!
Amen.

* *A.* is sung by *all* the Brethren; *Ch.* by the Choir; and *L.* by the Liturgist.

T. 146, 2d p.

*L.* Accept a weeping eye,
A warm and grateful heart,
Tho' a thank-off'ring poor,
Yet take it in good part.

T. 1.

*A.* Yea, turn in mercy, Lord, to us thy face;
We're indigent, enrich us with thy grace!

*L.**. With all the merits of thy life,
*A**. Blefs us, gracious Lord and God!
Thy holy incarnation and birth
Make our humanity dear to us!
Thy circumcifion
Effect in us the circumcifion of the heart!
Thy early exile
Teach us that we are pilgrims on earth!
By thy obedience and fubjection
Grant us obedient hearts!
Thy precious fweat, when at work,
Make all labor eafy unto us!
Thy faithfulnefs in handicraft bufinefs,
Make us faithful on our part!
Thy unfpotted youth
Sanctify the fingle brethren's ftate!

T. 56, 2d p.

*Sung.* Ev'ry hour and ev'ry where
May our words and actions bear
A refemblance, gracious Lord, to thine!

*L.* With thy agony and bloody fweat,
With thy bitter fufferings and death,
*A.* Blefs and comfort us, dear Lord and God!

* This is prayed alternately by the Liturgift and the Brethren.

T. 9.

T. 9.

*Sung.* Jeſus, who haſt us regain'd,
Faithful Lord and Savior,
Give us what thy death obtain'd,
And we're rich for ever.

*L.* Thy pierced hands
*A.* Show us where our names are written!
Thy ſuffering and dying form
Remain conſtantly before our eyes!
Thy ſacred, tormented body,
Mortify our members, which are on earth,
(Col. iii. 5.)
Thy heart pierced for us
Be joyful over us!

T. 582.

*Sung.* Jeſus, to thee we give
Ourſelves this day anew,
As thy reward ſo dearly gain'd,
Thy ſpoil and purchaſe due;
That with us thou may'ſt do,
What's pleaſing in thy ſight,
And from us take, whate'er thee grieves,
Whate'er thou think'ſt not right.

T. 539. a.

*L.* O thou Lamb of God, which takeſt away the ſin of the world,
*A.* Have mercy upon us!

*L.* O thou Lamb of God, which takeſt away the ſin of the world,
*A.* Own us to be thine!

*L.* O thou Lamb of God, which takeſt away the ſin of the world,
*A.* Leave thy peace with us!

T. 79.

*Sung.* O King of Peace, our Sov'reign,
Thou ſhalt alone us govern;
Come, form us ſoon to be
T' each other an example,
To th' Holy Ghoſt a temple,
To th' Father pleaſing conſtantly!

2. T. 235.

*Ch.* LORD God, thy praiſe we ſing,
*A.* To thee our thanks we bring,
Lord Jeſus Chriſt, we honor thee,
That thou vouchſaf'dſt a man to be,
And gav'ſt thyſelf a ſacrifice,
To pay for all a ranſom price;
This comforts us eternally,
And makes us hope for mercy free,
Amen.

T. 22. b.

*Lit.* 1. O word, which pow'r and comfort brings,
Whence pardon and ſalvation ſprings:
" *God deign'd a man like me to be,*
" *To ſhed his blood and die for me.*"

*A.* 2. O Lord, 'fore whom all creatures bow,
How could'ſt thou deign to ſtoop ſo low!

What

What is poor man, that thou ſhouldſt him
So highly value and eſteem?

*L.* In all things it behoved him to be made like unto his brethren, that he might be a merciful and faithful High-Prieſt in things pertaining to God; who can be touched with the feeling of our infirmities, and was in all points tempted like as we are, yet without ſin,

*Ch.* In that he himſelf hath ſuffered, being tempted, he is able to ſuccour them that are tempted.

T. 22. d.

*A.* 3. If Jeſus not our Savior were,
What could our hearts revive and cheer?
We have receiv'd a deadly wound,
There's nought in ſoul and body ſound.

*L.* O rejoice for evermore!
Jeſus beareth all your members;
The moſt helpleſs, weak, and poor
Of his brethren he remembers,
And thro' his humanity
Sanctifieth you and me.

T. 11. d.

*A.* 1. When we now explore the end,
Why our Lord would condeſcend
To aſſume humanity,
Us thereby to ſanctify;

*Ch.* 2. And reflect on all the pain,
Which for us he did ſuſtain,
On his labor, reſt and cares,
On his tears and fervent pray'rs,

3. Poverty and ev'ry want,
To our nature incident,

Which he bore, and which for us
All is meritorious:

*A.* 4. Then thro' his enabling grace
We with joy can run our race,
Whilst we him in mem'ry bear,
Who was tempted, as we are.

5. Praise to him for ever be,
We're his blood-bought property,
Since he death for us endur'd,
And eternal life procur'd.

*L.* Ye are bought with a price; therefore glorify God in your body and in your spirit, which are God's!

T. 235.

*A.* Jesus, our hearts to thee incline,
And may our minds resemble thine,
O'erstream us with the healing flood
Of thy divine atoning blood,
That soul and body may always
By word and deed show forth thy praise!
Amen.

3. T. 235.

*A.* GLORY and thanks to thee,
Jesus, for ever be,
Who, tho' th' eternal God,
Assum'dst our flesh and blood!

Ch.

*Ch.* Thrice happy are those souls indeed,
Who sowing tears, a precious seed,
Find in this world of woe and strife,
Pattern and comfort in thy life;
For this thy grace by us, O Lord!
Be humbly in the dust ador'd!
Amen.

T. 22. e.

1. Those blessings on us all bestow,
Which from thy holy merits flow,
Open to us this precious store,
Lord Jesus, and we ask no more.

T. 22. a.

2. We from thy toilsome life derive
Rich comforts while on earth we live;
*Ch.* Thou for our sake didst bear the cross,
And still with patience bear'st with us.

*A.* 3. By all that thou hast done or said,
Great blessings thou hast merited,
Thy walking, sleeping, toil, and sweat,
Redound unto our benefit.

T. 22. f.

4. In servant's form thou mad'st us free
From Satan's cruel tyranny.
Our chastisement on thee was laid,
Thy blood for us a ransom paid.

5. Our likeness thou didst still retain
Ascending into Heav'n again,
Where thee in glory we shall see,
And also be made like to thee.

T. 22. o.

6. Lord Jeſus Chriſt, all praiſe to thee,
That from the curſe we're now ſet free,
Since thou our curſe haſt borne, and thus
From ſin and guilt deliver'd us.

7. We pray thee, fix our hearts and eyes
Upon thy bleeding ſacrifice,
That we may day and night by faith
Enjoy the merits of thy death.

8. Grant, that it may to all appear,
That we thy death in mem'ry bear,
And may ev'n in our looks ſerene
Likeneſs of Chriſt, our friend, be ſeen.

T. 23.

*Ch.* That our minds and whole behavior
May reſemble thee our Savior,
And thy ſanctifying merit
Hallow body, ſoul, and ſpirit.

T. 22. d.

*A.* 9. In this world thou art no more now,
Us as thy race thou leav'ſt below;
Take us into thy ſpecial care,
Secure our ſouls from ev'ry ſnare.

10. Let our white robes of righteouſneſs
Be by thy blood kept clean always;
Thy whole ſalvation make our own,
And us with conſtant vict'ry crown!

T. 235.

*Ch.* 11. That name which only to thee's known,
Lay on our Choir, we are thine own,

And by thy incarnation bleſt,
Preſerve our ſouls and bodies chaſte.
Amen.

4. T. 121.

*L. & Ch.* O JESUS, ſource of grace,
Impart thy precious peace
To our Choir and Claſſes,
Whene'er we ſeek thy face,
When we, to give thee praiſes,
Humbly bow the knee,
And bring thanks to thee,
In ſweet harmony.

T. 29.

*A.* 1. Bleſs, Jeſus! with thy peace and favor
Our Choir, as oft as we endeavor,
T' exalt thy matchleſs love and grace,
And thee with thankful hearts to praiſe;

2. That thou, the God of our ſalvation,
Conſtrain'd by mercy and compaſſion,
Becam'ſt a man to ſet us free
From guilt, and curſe, and miſery.

3. Thanks for the inexhauſted treaſure
Of bleſſings, which in richeſt meaſure
From thee on us poor ſinners flow,
And prove our comfort here below.

*L. & Ch.* O precious thoughts of peace!
O undeſerved grace!
All of us had periſh'd
In ſins and treſpaſſes,

Hadſt

Hadſt thou not for us purchas'd
Life and ev'ry good,
By thy precious blood,
Jeſus, man and God!

*A.* 4. Jeſus, thy love and condeſcenſion
Is great beyond all comprehenſion;
Thou from the manger to the croſs
Gav'ſt countleſs proofs of love to us.

5. Thou boreſt our ſins and curſe-infliction,
For us to purchaſe benediction,
And didſt by conq'ring death and hell
Sin's power and dominion quell.

6. Thy words, thy walk, thy interceſſion,
Thy tears, thy cries, and bitter paſſion,
Yea, all that thou haſt done for us,
Is truly meritorious.

*L. & Ch.* This fills our hearts with joy;
We gladly teſtify
Of his great ſalvation,
And publiſh far and near
With deep humiliation,
That his blood divine
Can waſh ſinners clean,
From all ſtains of ſin.

*A.* 7. O may we at thy feet, dear Savior,
Still more enjoy thy grace and favor,
Conſtrain'd by thy redeeming love
May we thy true diſciples prove.

8. Our lives for thee O may we venture,
And freely in thy ſervice enter,
Yea, may our Choir ſhow forth thy praiſe
And honor thee in all their ways!

*L. & Ch.*

*L.* & *Ch.* Might each one in us trace
Th' effect of Jesu's grace,
That by him inspired
With zeal and willingness,
Each Brother's heart be fired,
Out of gratitude
To spend life and blood,
In the cause of God.

*A.* 9. In faith we say: Amen, Lord Jesus,
Unto our Choir be thou propitious,
And glorify thy name still more
In us, we humbly thee implore.

*L.* & *Ch.* 10. He'll grant it: Hearts and hands surrender
Anew to him, with love most tender,
And vow, that, till his face you see,
To him you will obedient be.

T. 159.

*A.* To Father, Son, and Holy Ghost,
Our God, we render praise!
In concert with the ransom'd host
We sing redeeming grace;
Whilst they, who round his throne appear,
The wonders of his love declare,
And sing: "The Lamb for us was slain:"
Our hearts reply: Amen.

# III.

## LITANIES OF THE SINGLE SISTERS.

### 1*. T. 235.

*A.* UNSPOTTED Lamb of God,
Our holy Spouſe by blood,
Who from thy throne cam'ſt down,
And took'ſt our fleſh and bone:
Thou, Lord, by dying on the croſs
Mad'ſt peace between our God and us;
Thy grace upon our Choir beſtow'd
Claims our unfeigned gratitude;
To thee our thanks we proſtrate bring,
And joyful Hallelujah ſing.
Amen.

T. 50.

1. Jeſus, all praiſe is due to thee,
That thou wert pleas'd a man to be,
Born of a Virgin. Now rejoice,
Ye virgins, both with heart and voice,
Hallelujah!

2. O did each pulſe thankſgiving beat,
And every breath thy praiſe repeat

* *A.* is ſung by the Siſters; *Ch.* by the Chorus; and *L.* by the Liturgiſt.

For thy birth, ſuff'rings, wounds, and death,
Whereon we humbly truſt by faith.
Hallelujah!

*Ch.* 3. O wonder without parallel,
O grace divine unſearchable,
Myſt'ry of godlineſs, which we
Can ne'er extol ſufficiently.
Hallelujah!

*L.* 4. For us theſe wonders he hath wrought,
To ſhow his love ſurpaſſing thought.
Ye, who are his, be glad and ſing
Praiſe to our Savior, God, and King:
*A.* Hallelujah!

T. 249. 2d p.

Thou holy bleſſed Trinity,
For th' Lamb of God all praiſe to thee!
Amen, Hallelujah!
*Ch.* Hallelujah!
*A.* Amen, Hallelujah!

T. 22. b.

5. O might we to our gracious Lord
For all his goodneſs joy afford!
Each virgin's care and aim be this,
To ſeek in all things him to pleaſe.

6. Abide with us, on thee we call,
Jeſus, thou art our ALL in ALL;
Let us, devoted unto thee,
In ſoul and body hallow'd be!

7. May we uninterruptedly
In ſweet communion live with thee,
Till we have finiſh'd here our race,
*And ſhall behold thee face to face.*

T. 58.

T. 58. 2d p.

*L.* Now then wait with longing and perſevering
For Jeſus, that you may at his appearing
Meet him with joy.

O may he preſerve you in ſoul and body,
Unblemiſh'd, and with him in union ſteady,
Until he comes.

*A.* Amen: Lord, afford us thy kind direction,
Keep us from evil, and in thy protection
Always ſecure;

Till we ſhall in Heaven behold thy glory,
And freed from ſin and weakneſs there adore thee
World without end.

2. T. 235.

*A.* PRAISE God, the Father, Son,
And Spirit, three in one,
For that decree of love and grace
To ſave from death the human race,
By Jeſu's human birth for us,
Suff'rings, and dying on the croſs.
For this our choir doth him adore
With grateful hearts for evermore.
Amen.

T. 22. b.

1. O Abba, Father, thanks and praiſe
And joyful ſongs to thee we raiſe,

That thou thy Son out of thy throne
Didſt give, to be a Virgin's ſon:

2. And turn'ſt thy all-reviving face,
Unto our poverty in grace,
*Ch.* Own'ſt us in thy beloved Son,
Whoſe blood did for our ſins atone.

*A.* 3. We feel thy kind paternal heart
To us, who have in Chriſt a part,
And Jeſu's blood and righteouſneſs
Our ſplendor is, our glorious dreſs.

T. 22. o.

4. God Holy Ghoſt, we praiſe thy name,
With rev'rence we thy love proclaim,
That overſhadow'd by thy pow'r
The Virgin Chriſt conceiv'd and bore.

5. He died for us; and thou from hence
Salvation doſt to us diſpenſe,
And to the glory of his grace
Work'ſt in us fruits of righteouſneſs.

6. Fix in our hearts thy bleſt abode,
And make us temples of our God;
*L.* Keep ſoul and body, through thy care,
Blameleſs, until the Lord appear.

T. 22. d.

*A.* 7. Thou, who the wondrous deed haſt done,
O Jeſu, look in mercy down
On us, altho' we ſinners be
Void of angelic purity.

*Ch.* 8. Like Mary, we with heart and voice
In thee our Savior will rejoice;
*A.* Since thou haſt promiſed in grace,
To make our hearts thy dwelling place.

*L.* 9. Grant, that each virgin's countenance
This bleſt experience may evince;
In ev'ry handmaid's look be ſeen
The poor one of the Lord within.

T. 235.

*A.* O Lamb of God, Lord Jeſus Chriſt,
The bridegroom of thy Church confeſt,
Our Choir we now commend to thee,
Preſerve us thine eternally;
Form us according to thy mind,
To follow thee make us inclin'd,
That we may not confounded be,
When thou ſhalt come in majeſty.
Amen.

3. T. 235.

*A.* THOU, Lord, faithful and true!
Whoſe grace is daily new,
With mercies numberleſs
Doſt ſoul and body bleſs!
We can't expreſs ſufficiently
Our gratitude and love to thee.
*Ch.* Thou haſt by blood for us aton'd,
Us with thy tender mercies crown'd,
*A.* And wilt continue ev'ry day
To do more than we think and pray:

This we believe, and wait to see
The bleſt fulfilment, Lord, from thee.
Amen.

*L.* With all the merits of thy life, ſufferings, and death,
*A.* *Bleſs us, our dear Lord and God!*

T. 9.

*Sung.* Grant, that we alone from thee,
Well-ſpring of ſalvation,
May for ſoul and body gain
True ſanctification.

*L**. Thy becoming man in a Virgin's womb,
*A**. *Render the Virgins chaſte!*
Thy child-like ſimplicity,
*Effect in us ſingleneſs of heart and mind!*
Thy weakneſs and infirmity,
*Make us contented with our weakneſs!*
Thy blood-ſweat in thy agony,
*Bedew our ſouls and bodies!*
Thy pierced hands,
*Show us where our names are written!*
Thy pierced feet
*Are embraced by us for our election of grace!*
Thy gracious lips, pale in death,
*Speak peace and comfort to our hearts!*
Thy ſuff'ring and dying form,
*Remain always before our eyes!*
Thy heart pierced for us
*Be joyful over us!*

T. 168. b. 2d p.

*Sung.* Form thyſelf our virgin claſſes,
So unto thy praiſe, Lord Jeſus,

* This is prayed alternately by the Liturgiſt and all the Siſters.

That

That thou may'st, till we depart,
Find in each a faithful heart.

*L.* With thy coming again unto thy Church, or our being called home to thee,
*A.* *Comfort us, dear Lord and God!*

T. 22. f.

1. In spirit we behold with joy
That blest triumphant company,
The Church, redeemed by Christ's blood
And perfected, which seeth God.

2. Daily the blessed Comforter
Keeps us in fellowship with her,
And fills our hearts with tender love
To Christ, till we're with him above.

T. 588.

*Ch.* Now ready stand
Ye virgins, ready stand;
The Bridegroom is at hand:
Sleep not, nor slumber,
Let nothing you encumber,
But ready stand;
He is at hand.

T. 22. d.

*A.* 3. Meanwhile our Choir's concern shall be
To follow him continually,
To him each day in faith to cleave,
And to his joy and praise to live.

4. Thus he will still most graciously
Regard our tears and poverty,

Which

Which often raiſes in our breaſt
That wiſh, to be with him at reſt.

T. 235.

While we enjoy his love and peace,
His humbling and exalting grace:
This ſweetly can alleviate
The pain his abſence doth create,
And we, in ſoul and body bleſt,
Thus glorify the name of Chriſt.
Amen!

## 4.

*L. & Ch.* PRAISE ye the Lord, for he is good, ſing praiſes unto his name, for it is pleaſant.

T. 58. 2d p.

*A.* *Sacred name of Jeſus,*
So great and holy,
That all our tongues can never praiſe thee truly
As thou deſerv'ſt.

T. 249, 2d p.

*L. & Ch.* O might our virgin choirs proclaim
By word and deed his ſaving name!
Might they in all their ways,
Led by his grace,
Show forth his matchleſs praiſe!

*A.* *Pow'rful name of Jeſus,*
Thou'rt efficacious,
To ſave, to ſanctiſy, and to preſerve us;
Thee we adore.

*L. & Ch.*

*L.* & *Ch.* Lord Jesus! praise and thanks to thee,
If thou wert not, what shou'd we be?
Thy saving name we bless,
And thee confess
Source of our happiness.

*A.* *Precious name of Jesus,*
How sweet and blessed
Art thou to souls, who mourning and distressed
Upon thee call.

*L.* & *Ch.* With him my heart hath always found
True counsel, comfort, help abound,
Therefore I will rely
Eternally
On his fidelity.

*A.* *Glad'ning name of Jesus,*
Whence comfort floweth,
No angel like a contrite sinner knoweth
Thy pow'r divine.

*L.* & *Ch.* All misery, however great,
His comforts can alleviate;
Therefore in all distress
Seek ye his face,
And humbly sue for grace.

*A.* *Loveliest name of Jesus,*
Whoe'er confideth
In thee, obtains a treasure, which abideth.
Hallelujah!

*L.* & *Ch.* If I have him, I have howe'er,
What me eternally can cheer;

All

All in his name implied
Is verified,
His grace be magnified.

*A.* Now let all ſay: Amen,
*The Lord be praiſed,*
*And Jeſu's ſaving name be ever bleſſed:*
Hallelujah!

*Ch.* Amen, Hallelujah!
Hallelujah!
*A.* Amen, Hallelujah!

---

# IV.

## LITANIES OF THE MARRIED BRETHREN AND SISTERS.

### 1 *. T. 235.

*L. & Ch.* O CHOIR, brought nigh to God
By Chriſt's atoning blood,
Unto the triune God draw near
With tender love and filial fear,
With tears of heart-felt gratitude,
With ſoul and body deeply bow'd;
And to the Father and the Son,
And Holy Spirit, three in one,
Thy praiſes and thank-off'rings bring,
And holy, holy, holy ſing.
Amen.

T. 4.

*A.* Receive at thy throne,
O Father and Son,
And Spirit of grace,
In Jeſu's name, honor, thankſgiving, and praiſe.

* Whatever in theſe Litanies is marked with *A*, is ſung by the whole Choir; *B.* by the Brethren; *S.* by the Siſters; *Ch.* by the Chorus; and *L.* by the Liturgiſt.

*L.* Our Lord Chriſt Jeſus,
*A.* Be gracious unto us!
*L.* O thou God and Father of the Church,
*A.* Preſerve us in thy love!
*L.* Lord God, Holy Ghoſt,
*A.* Maintain thy temple in ſanctification and honor!

T. 249. 2d p.

Moſt holy bleſſed Trinity!
We praiſe thee to eternity,
*Ch.* Amen, Hallelujah! Hallelujah!
*A.* Amen, Hallelujah!

T. 22. b.

1. Father, we daily worſhip thee,
As Chriſt's redeemed property,
*S.* That thou thy Son, out of thy throne,
Didſt give to be a Virgin's Son.

*A.* 2. O grant, that we may all, while here,
In his ſalvation fully ſhare,
And ſanctify our married ſtate,
As thy own work, we thee entreat.

T. 22. e.

*A.* 3. O Spirit, who all hearts doſt try,
And ſoul and body purify,
*S.* O'erſhadow'd by whoſe mighty pow'r
The Virgin Chriſt conceiv'd and bore;

4. Make our whole Choir thy bleſt abode,
A temple of the living God,
Teach us to know Chriſt's mind, and keep
Us all with him in fellowſhip.

T. 22. o.

5. Lord Jesus, evermore ador'd,
*L. & Ch.* Thy body's Savior, head, and Lord!
*A.* No words can e'er our thankfulness
And heart-felt joy in thee express,

6. That thou, the whole creation's God,
Assumd'st our feeble flesh and blood,
And by thy death didst set us free
From endless woe and misery.

T. 22. f.

7. Those blessings on us all bestow,
Which from thy life and suff'rings flow,
And grant us fully to enjoy
All thou hast merited thereby.

T. 22. l.

8. O may each soul and ev'ry pair
In their whole walk thy praise declare,
And here on earth invariably
In sweet communion live with thee.

9. O may we yield thee joy and feel,
That thou amongst us deign'st to dwell,
*L. & Ch.* Though we can't see thee with our eyes,
Our faith the want of sight supplies.

T. 9.

*A.* If thou'rt with us, then indeed,
We shall lack no blessing,
But with thee, O Christ, proceed,
To meet joys unceasing.

May our Children, gracious Lord,
Share with us thy favor;

Let them all be the reward
Of thy death for ever.

T. 185.

*L.* The Lord bleſs and keep thee in his favor,
As his choſen property;
The Lord make his face ſhine on thee ever,
And be gracious unto thee!
The Lord lift his countenance moſt gracious
Upon thee, and be to thee propitious,
And his peace on thee beſtow!
*A.* Amen, Amen, be it ſo!

2. T. 235.

*A.* AMEN, Hallelujah!
*B.* Glory, and pow'r, and ſway,
*S.* Worſhip, thankſgiving, praiſe,
*A.* With ſongs and ſolemn lays,
Be brought to Chriſt, who by his blood
Made us acceptable to God;
Tho' conſcious of our poverty,
Of faults, defects, and miſery,
Yet cloathed in the glorious dreſs
Of Jeſu's blood-bought righteouſneſs,
With confidence and filial fear
We to the triune God draw near,
From whom, ſince we in Chriſt believe,
Grace, peace, and bleſſing we receive.
Amen.

T. 22. b.

1. O Father, who didſt ſend thy Son
To us from thy celeſtial throne,

These

Thoſe bleſſings on our Choir beſtow,
Which from his holy merits flow.

2. That we may in this preſent time
On earth one ſpirit be with him,
S. That all in us his mind may trace,
A. And we thro' him ſhow forth thy praiſe.

T. 22. d.

3. Jeſus, who ſav'dſt us by thy croſs,
B. From whom thro' faith our comfort flows;
A. In mercy, Lord, on us look down,
Since thou didſt for our ſins atone.

T. 22. l.

4. We worſhip thee with awe, and kiſs
Thy pierced feet with heart-felt bliſs;
B. We are thy ſervants thro' thy grace,
S. Ourſelves thy handmaids we confeſs,

A. 5. And thou art our moſt gracious Lord,
To whom we fain wou'd joy afford;
Let us be guided by thy hand:
Then bleſſing will our courſe attend.

T. 22. o.

6. O purify our ſouls, we pray,
Thro' thy bleſt Spirit, to obey
The truth, and thus our faith to prove
By brotherly unfeigned love.

7. O may our mortal bodies be
Devoted, Jeſus, unto thee,
An holy living ſacrifice
To God, and pleaſing in his eyes!

Which he bore, and which for us
All is meritorious:

*A.* 4. Then thro' his enabling grace
We with joy can run our race,
Whilst we him in mem'ry bear,
Who was tempted, as we are.

5. Praise to him for ever be,
We're his blood-bought property,
Since he death for us endur'd,
And eternal life procur'd.

*L.* Ye are bought with a price; therefore glorify God in your body and in your spirit, which are God's!

T. 235.

*A.* Jesus, our hearts to thee incline,
And may our minds resemble thine,
O'erstream us with the healing flood
Of thy divine atoning blood,
That soul and body may always
By word and deed show forth thy praise!
Amen.

3. T. 235.

*A.* GLORY and thanks to thee,
Jesus, for ever be,
Who, tho' th' eternal God,
Assum'dst our flesh and blood!

*Ch.* Thrice happy are those souls indeed,
Who sowing tears, a precious seed,
Find in this world of woe and strife,
Pattern and comfort in thy life;
For this thy grace by us, O Lord!
Be humbly in the dust ador'd!
Amen.

T. 22. e.

1. Those blessings on us all bestow,
Which from thy holy merits flow,
Open to us this precious store,
Lord Jesus, and we ask no more.

T. 22. a.

2. We from thy toilsome life derive
Rich comforts while on earth we live;
*Ch.* Thou for our sake didst bear the cross,
And still with patience bear'st with us.

*A.* 3. By all that thou hast done or said,
Great blessings thou hast merited,
Thy walking, sleeping, toil, and sweat,
Redound unto our benefit.

T. 22. f.

4. In servant's form thou mad'st us free
From Satan's cruel tyranny.
Our chastisement on thee was laid,
Thy blood for us a ransom paid.

5. Our likeness thou didst still retain
Ascending into Heav'n again,
Where thee in glory we shall see,
And also be made like to thee.

T. 22. o.

6. Lord Jesus Christ, all praise to thee,
That from the curse we're now set free,
Since thou our curse hast borne, and thus
From sin and guilt deliver'd us.

7. We pray thee, fix our hearts and eyes
Upon thy bleeding sacrifice,
That we may day and night by faith
Enjoy the merits of thy death.

8. Grant, that it may to all appear,
That we thy death in mem'ry bear,
And may ev'n in our looks serene
Likeness of Christ, our friend, be seen.

T. 23.

*Ch.* That our minds and whole behavior
May resemble thee our Savior,
And thy sanctifying merit
Hallow body, soul, and spirit.

T. 22. d.

*A.* 9. In this world thou art no more now,
Us as thy race thou leav'st below;
Take us into thy special care,
Secure our souls from ev'ry snare.

10. Let our white robes of righteousness
Be by thy blood kept clean always;
Thy whole salvation make our own,
And us with constant vict'ry crown!

T. 235.

*Ch.* 11. That name which only to thee's known,
Lay on our Choir, we are thine own,

And by thy incarnation bleſt,
Preſerve our ſouls and bodies chaſte.
Amen.

4. T. 121.

*L. & Ch.* O JESUS, ſource of grace,
Impart thy precious peace
To our Choir and Claſſes,
Whene'er we ſeek thy face,
When we, to give thee praiſes,
Humbly bow the knee,
And bring thanks to thee,
In ſweet harmony.

T. 29.

*A.* 1. Bleſs, Jeſus! with thy peace and favor
Our Choir, as oft as we endeavor,
T' exalt thy matchleſs love and grace,
And thee with thankful hearts to praiſe;

2. That thou, the God of our ſalvation,
Conſtrain'd by mercy and compaſſion,
Becam'ſt a man to ſet us free
From guilt, and curſe, and miſery.

3. Thanks for the inexhauſted treaſure
Of bleſſings, which in richeſt meaſure
From thee on us poor ſinners flow,
And prove our comfort here below.

*L. & Ch.* O precious thoughts of peace!
O undeſerved grace!
All of us had periſh'd
In ſins and treſpaſſes,

Hadſt

Hadſt thou not for us purchas'd
Life and ev'ry good,
By thy precious blood,
Jeſus, man and God!

*A.* 4. Jeſus, thy love and condeſcenſion
Is great beyond all comprehenſion;
Thou from the manger to the croſs
Gav'ſt countleſs proofs of love to us.

5. Thou boreſt our ſins and curſe-infliction,
For us to purchaſe benediction,
And didſt by conq'ring death and hell
Sin's power and dominion quell.

6. Thy words, thy walk, thy interceſſion,
Thy tears, thy cries, and bitter paſſion,
Yea, all that thou haſt done for us,
Is truly meritorious.

*L. & Ch.* This fills our hearts with joy;
We gladly teſtify
Of his great ſalvation,
And publiſh far and near
With deep humiliation,
That his blood divine
Can waſh ſinners clean,
From all ſtains of ſin.

*A.* 7. O may we at thy feet, dear Savior,
Still more enjoy thy grace and favor,
Conſtrain'd by thy redeeming love
May we thy true diſciples prove.

8. Our lives for thee O may we venture,
And freely in thy ſervice enter,
Yea, may our Choir ſhow forth thy praiſe
And honor thee in all their ways!

*L. & Ch.*

*L.* & *Ch.* Might each one in us trace
Th' effect of Jesu's grace,
That by him inspired
With zeal and willingness,
Each Brother's heart be fired,
Out of gratitude
To spend life and blood,
In the cause of God.

*A.* 9. In faith we say: Amen, Lord Jesus,
Unto our Choir be thou propitious,
And glorify thy name still more
In us, we humbly thee implore.

*L.* & *Ch.* 10. He'll grant it: Hearts and hands surrender
Anew to him, with love most tender,
And vow, that, till his face you see,
To him you will obedient be.

T. 159.

*A.* To Father, Son, and Holy Ghost,
Our God, we render praise!
In concert with the ransom'd host
We sing redeeming grace;
Whilst they, who round his throne appear,
The wonders of his love declare,
And sing: "The Lamb for us was slain:"
Our hearts reply: Amen.



## III.

## LITANIES OF THE SINGLE SISTERS.

### 1*. T. 235.

*A.* UNSPOTTED Lamb of God,
Our holy Spouſe by blood,
Who from thy throne cam'ſt down,
And took'ſt our fleſh and bone:
Thou, Lord, by dying on the croſs
Mad'ſt peace between our God and us;
Thy grace upon our Choir beſtow'd
Claims our unfeigned gratitude;
To thee our thanks we proſtrate bring,
And joyful Hallelujah ſing.
Amen.

T. 50.

1. Jeſus, all praiſe is due to thee,
That thou wert pleas'd a man to be,
Born of a Virgin. Now rejoice,
Ye virgins, both with heart and voice,
Hallelujah!

2. O did each pulſe thankſgiving beat,
And every breath thy praiſe repeat

* *A.* is ſung by the Siſters; *Ch.* by the Chorus; and *L.* by the Liturgiſt.

For thy birth, ſuff'rings, wounds, and death,
Whereon we humbly truſt by faith.
Hallelujah!

*Ch.* 3. O wonder without parallel,
O grace divine unſearchable,
Myſt'ry of godlineſs, which we
Can ne'er extol ſufficiently.
Hallelujah!

*L.* 4. For us theſe wonders he hath wrought,
To ſhow his love ſurpaſſing thought.
Ye, who are his, be glad and ſing
Praiſe to our Savior, God, and King:
*A.* Hallelujah!

T. 249. 2d p.

Thou holy bleſſed Trinity,
For th' Lamb of God all praiſe to thee!
Amen, Hallelujah!
*Ch.* Hallelujah!
*A.* Amen, Hallelujah!

T. 22. b.

5. O might we to our gracious Lord
For all his goodneſs joy afford!
Each virgin's care and aim be this,
To ſeek in all things him to pleaſe.

6. Abide with us, on thee we call,
Jeſus, thou art our ALL in ALL;
Let us, devoted unto thee,
In ſoul and body hallow'd be!

7. May we uninterruptedly
In ſweet communion live with thee,
Till we have finiſh'd here our race,
*And ſhall behold thee face to face.*

T. 58. 2d p.

*L.* Now then wait with longing and perſevering
For Jeſus, that you may at his appearing
Meet him with joy.

O may he preſerve you in ſoul and body,
Unblemiſh'd, and with him in union ſteady,
Until he comes.

*A.* Amen: Lord, afford us thy kind direction,
Keep us from evil, and in thy protection
Always ſecure;

Till we ſhall in Heaven behold thy glory,
And freed from ſin and weakneſs there adore thee
World without end.

2. T. 235.

*A.* PRAISE God, the Father, Son,
And Spirit, three in one,
For that decree of love and grace
To ſave from death the human race,
By Jeſu's human birth for us,
Suff'rings, and dying on the croſs.
For this our choir doth him adore
With grateful hearts for evermore.
Amen.

T. 22. b.

1. O Abba, Father, thanks and praiſe
And joyful ſongs to thee we raiſe,

That thou thy Son out of thy throne
Didſt give, to be a Virgin's ſon:

2. And turn'ſt thy all-reviving face,
Unto our poverty in grace,
*Ch.* Own'ſt us in thy beloved Son,
Whoſe blood did for our ſins atone.

*A.* 3. We feel thy kind paternal heart
To us, who have in Chriſt a part,
And Jeſu's blood and righteouſneſs
Our ſplendor is, our glorious dreſs.

T. 22. o.

4. God Holy Ghoſt, we praiſe thy name,
With rev'rence we thy love proclaim,
That overſhadow'd by thy pow'r
The Virgin Chriſt conceiv'd and bore.

5. He died for us; and thou from hence
Salvation doſt to us diſpenſe,
And to the glory of his grace
Work'ſt in us fruits of righteouſneſs.

6. Fix in our hearts thy bleſt abode,
And make us temples of our God;
*L.* Keep ſoul and body, through thy care,
Blameleſs, until the Lord appear.

T. 22. d.

*A.* 7. Thou, who the wondrous deed haſt done,
O Jeſu, look in mercy down
On us, altho' we ſinners be
Void of angelic purity.

*Ch.* 8.

*Ch.* 8. Like Mary, we with heart and voice
In thee our Savior will rejoice;
*A.* Since thou haſt promiſed in grace,
To make our hearts thy dwelling place.

*L.* 9. Grant, that each virgin's countenance
This bleſt experience may evince;
In ev'ry handmaid's look be ſeen
The poor one of the Lord within.

T. 235.

*A.* O Lamb of God, Lord Jeſus Chriſt,
The bridegroom of thy Church confeſt,
Our Choir we now commend to thee,
Preſerve us thine eternally;
Form us according to thy mind,
To follow thee make us inclin'd,
That we may not confounded be,
When thou ſhalt come in majeſty.
Amen.

3. T. 235.

*A.* THOU, Lord, faithful and true!
Whoſe grace is daily new,
With mercies numberleſs
Doſt ſoul and body bleſs!
We can't expreſs ſufficiently
Our gratitude and love to thee.
*Ch.* Thou haſt by blood for us aton'd,
Us with thy tender mercies crown'd,
*A.* And wilt continue ev'ry day
To do more than we think and pray:

This we believe, and wait to see
The blest fulfilment, Lord, from thee.
Amen.

*L.* With all the merits of thy life, sufferings, and death,
*A.* *Bless us, our dear Lord and God!*

T. 9.

*Sung.* Grant, that we alone from thee,
Well-spring of salvation,
May for soul and body gain
True sanctification.

*L**. Thy becoming man in a Virgin's womb,
*A**. *Render the Virgins chaste!*
Thy child-like simplicity,
*Effect in us singleness of heart and mind!*
Thy weakness and infirmity,
*Make us contented with our weakness!*
Thy blood-sweat in thy agony,
*Bedew our souls and bodies!*
Thy pierced hands,
*Show us where our names are written!*
Thy pierced feet
*Are embraced by us for our election of grace!*
Thy gracious lips, pale in death,
*Speak peace and comfort to our hearts!*
Thy suff'ring and dying form,
*Remain always before our eyes!*
Thy heart pierced for us
*Be joyful over us!*

T. 168. b. 2d p.

*Sung.* Form thyself our virgin classes,
So unto thy praise, Lord Jesus,

* This is prayed alternately by the Liturgist and all the Sisters.

That

That thou may'ſt, till we depart,
Find in each a faithful heart.

*L.* With thy coming again unto thy Church, or our being called home to thee,
*A.* *Comfort us, dear Lord and God!*

T. 22. f.

1. In ſpirit we behold with joy
That bleſt triumphant company,
The Church, redeemed by Chriſt's blood
And perfected, which ſeeth God.

2. Daily the bleſſed Comforter
Keeps us in fellowſhip with her,
And fills our hearts with tender love
To Chriſt, till we're with him above.

T. 588.

*Ch.* Now ready ſtand
Ye virgins, ready ſtand;
The Bridegroom is at hand:
Sleep not, nor ſlumber,
Let nothing you encumber,
But ready ſtand;
He is at hand.

T. 22. d.

*A.* 3. Meanwhile our Choir's concern ſhall be
To follow him continually,
To him each day in faith to cleave,
And to his joy and praiſe to live.

4. Thus he will ſtill moſt graciouſly
Regard our tears and poverty,

Which

Which often raiſes in our breaſt
That wiſh, to be with him at reſt.

T. 235.

While we enjoy his love and peace,
His humbling and exalting grace:
This ſweetly can alleviate
The pain his abſence doth create,
And we, in ſoul and body bleſt,
Thus glorify the name of Chriſt.
Amen!

## 4.

*L. & Ch.* PRAISE ye the Lord, for he is good, ſing praiſes unto his name, for it is pleaſant.

T. 58. 2d p.

*A.* *Sacred name of Jeſus,*
So great and holy,
That all our tongues can never praiſe thee truly
As thou deſerv'ſt.

T. 249, 2d p.

*L. & Ch.* O might our virgin choirs proclaim
By word and deed his ſaving name!
Might they in all their ways,
Led by his grace,
Show forth his matchleſs praiſe!

*A.* *Pow'rful name of Jeſus,*
Thou'rt efficacious,
To ſave, to ſanctify, and to preſerve us;
Thee we adore.

*L. & Ch.*

*L. & Ch.* Lord Jesus! praise and thanks to thee,
If thou wert not, what shou'd we be?
Thy saving name we bless,
And thee confess
Source of our happiness.

*A.* *Precious name of Jesus,*
How sweet and blessed
Art thou to souls, who mourning and distressed
Upon thee call.

*L. & Ch.* With him my heart hath always found
True counsel, comfort, help abound,
Therefore I will rely
Eternally
On his fidelity.

*A.* *Glad'ning name of Jesus,*
Whence comfort floweth,
No angel like a contrite sinner knoweth
Thy pow'r divine.

*L. & Ch.* All misery, however great,
His comforts can alleviate;
Therefore in all distress
Seek ye his face,
And humbly sue for grace.

*A.* *Loveliest name of Jesus,*
Whoe'er confideth
In thee, obtains a treasure, which abideth.
Hallelujah!

*L. & Ch.* If I have him, I have howe'er,
What me eternally can cheer;

All

All in his name implied
Is verified,
His grace be magnified.

*A.* Now let all say: Amen,
*The Lord be praised,*
*And Jesu's saving name be ever blessed:*
Hallelujah!

*Ch.* Amen, Hallelujah!
Hallelujah!
*A.* Amen, Hallelujah!

---

## IV.

# LITANIES OF THE MARRIED BRETHREN AND SISTERS.

### 1 *. T. 235.

*L. & Ch.* O CHOIR, brought nigh to God
By Chriſt's atoning blood,
Unto the triune God draw near
With tender love and filial fear,
With tears of heart-felt gratitude,
With ſoul and body deeply bow'd;
And to the Father and the Son,
And Holy Spirit, three in one,
Thy praiſes and thank-off'rings bring,
And holy, holy, holy ſing.
Amen.

T. 4.

*A.* Receive at thy throne,
O Father and Son,
And Spirit of grace,
In Jeſu's name, honor, thankſgiving, and praiſe.

* Whatever in theſe Litanies is marked with *A*, is ſung by the whole Choir; *B*. by the Brethren; *S*. by the Siſters; *Ch*. by the Chorus; and *L*. by the Liturgiſt.

*L.* Our Lord Chriſt Jeſus,
*A.* Be gracious unto us!
*L.* O thou God and Father of the Church,
*A.* Preſerve us in thy love!
*L.* Lord God, Holy Ghoſt,
*A.* Maintain thy temple in ſanctification and honor

T. 249. 2d p.

Moſt holy bleſſed Trinity!
We praiſe thee to eternity,
*Ch.* Amen, Hallelujah! Hallelujah!
*A.* Amen, Hallelujah!

T. 22. b.

1. Father, we daily worſhip thee,
As Chriſt's redeemed property,
*S.* That thou thy Son, out of thy throne,
Didſt give to be a Virgin's Son.

*A.* 2. O grant, that we may all, while here,
In his ſalvation fully ſhare,
And ſanctify our married ſtate,
As thy own work, we thee entreat.

T. 22. e.

*A.* 3. O Spirit, who all hearts doſt try,
And ſoul and body purify,
*S.* O'erſhadow'd by whoſe mighty pow'r
The Virgin Chriſt conceiv'd and bore;

4. Make our whole Choir thy bleſt abode,
A temple of the living God,
Teach us to know Chriſt's mind, and keep
Us all with him in fellowſhip.

T. 22.

T. 22. o.

5. Lord Jesus, evermore ador'd,
*L.* & *Ch.* Thy body's Savior, head, and Lord!
*A.* No words can e'er our thankfulness
And heart-felt joy in thee express,

6. That thou, the whole creation's God,
Assumd'st our feeble flesh and blood,
And by thy death didst set us free
From endless woe and misery.

T. 22. f.

7. Those blessings on us all bestow,
Which from thy life and suff'rings flow,
And grant us fully to enjoy
All thou hast merited thereby.

T. 22. l.

8. O may each soul and ev'ry pair
In their whole walk thy praise declare,
And here on earth invariably
In sweet communion live with thee.

9. O may we yield thee joy and feel,
That thou amongst us deign'st to dwell,
*L.* & *Ch.* Though we can't see thee with our eyes,
Our faith the want of sight supplies.

T. 9.

*A.* If thou'rt with us, then indeed,
We shall lack no blessing,
But with thee, O Christ, proceed,
To meet joys unceasing.

May our Children, gracious Lord,
Share with us thy favor;

Let them all be the reward
Of thy death for ever.

T. 185.

*L.* The Lord bleſs and keep thee in his favor,
As his choſen property;
The Lord make his face ſhine on thee ever,
And be gracious unto thee!
The Lord lift his countenance moſt gracious
Upon thee, and be to thee propitious,
And his peace on thee beſtow!
*A.* Amen, Amen, be it ſo!

2. T. 235.

*A.* AMEN, Hallelujah!
*B.* Glory, and pow'r, and ſway,
*S.* Worſhip, thankſgiving, praiſe,
*A.* With ſongs and ſolemn lays,
Be brought to Chriſt, who by his blood
Made us acceptable to God;
Tho' conſcious of our poverty,
Of faults, defects, and miſery,
Yet cloathed in the glorious dreſs
Of Jeſu's blood-bought righteouſneſs,
With confidence and filial fear
We to the triune God draw near,
From whom, ſince we in Chriſt believe,
Grace, peace, and bleſſing we receive.
Amen.

T. 22. b.

1. O Father, who didſt ſend thy Son
To us from thy celeſtial throne,

These

Those blessings on our Choir bestow,
Which from his holy merits flow.

2. That we may in this present time
On earth one spirit be with him,
*S.* That all in us his mind may trace,
*A.* And we thro' him show forth thy praise.

T. 22. d.

3. Jesus, who sav'dst us by thy cross,
*B.* From whom thro' faith our comfort flows;
*A.* In mercy, Lord, on us look down,
Since thou didst for our sins atone.

T. 22. l.

4. We worship thee with awe, and kiss
Thy pierced feet with heart-felt bliss;
*B.* We are thy servants thro' thy grace,
S. Ourselves thy handmaids we confess,

*A.* 5. And thou art our most gracious Lord,
To whom we fain wou'd joy afford;
Let us be guided by thy hand:
Then blessing will our course attend.

T. 22. o.

6. O purify our souls, we pray,
Thro' thy blest Spirit, to obey
The truth, and thus our faith to prove
By brotherly unfeigned love.

7. O may our mortal bodies be
Devoted, Jesus, unto thee,
An holy living sacrifice
To God, and pleasing in his eyes!

T. 22. e.

8. Thou pow'r divine, God Holy Ghoſt,
*S.* Who all good gifts on us beſtow'ſt;
*B.* Who mak'ſt believers thine abode,
And temples of the living God;

*A.* 9. Keep us in ſoul and body clean,
*B.* Free from the pow'r and pain of ſin,
*S.* Our inward man ſo beautify,
That we may yield our Savior joy.

T. 22. f.

*A.* 10. Unto our Children grace afford,
That they may proſper for the Lord,
And our ſincere endeavors bleſs,
To train them up unto his praiſe.

T. 235.

Moſt holy Trinity, may they
And we, in all things thee obey,
Thro' Jeſu's grace yield thee delight,
And do what's pleaſing in thy ſight.
O may our Choir thy truth and grace
Experience till the end of days.
Amen!

3. T. 235.

*A.* THEE, God of love and peace, (2 Cor. xiii. 11.)
We magnify and praiſe,
Jeſus, who on the croſs
Didſt bleed and die for us:
*S.* In thy ſalvation we rejoice,
*B.* And give thee praiſe with heart and voice,
*A.* Conſcious, that all the happineſs,
We in the married ſtate poſſeſs,
Flows ſolely, gracious Lord, from thee,
For this thy name we glorify.
Amen.

T. 22. b.

*S.* 1. That thou from Heav'n to us didſt come,
And human fleſh and blood aſſume,
*B.* That thou didſt death for us endure,
For us ſalvation to procure.

*S.* 2. That Abba, whoſe dear Son thou art,
Our God and Father is declar'd,
*B.* That th' Holy Ghoſt makes us to be
One Spirit even here with thee.

T. 22. o.

*A.* 3. That thou the holy married ſtate,
(Ordain'd, when thou didſt man create,)
Haſt hallow'd by becoming man,
That we God's purpoſe might attain,

*L. & Ch.* 4. Thee and thy Church to repreſent,
And to fulfil thy bleſt intent,
To God a fruitful field to be,
T' increaſe thy blood-bought property:

T. 22. e.

*A.* 5. For this our hearts to thee we raiſe
With thankfulneſs, and give thee praiſe;
Might we and all our children, Lord,
In all things joy to thee afford!

T. 22. d.

6. Thy ſanctifying grace beſtow,
And be with us, where'er we go:
Thus ev'ry thing we do will be
Hallow'd and pleaſing unto thee.

T. 22. l.

7. Since thou, O Lord, with thine own hand
Haſt tied our ſacred marriage-band,
Grant, that thy dying love may be
The ſource of our felicity.

*S.* 8. Our ſouls and bodies, Lamb of God,
Beſprinkle with thy precious blood,
*B.* Subdue what's carnal by thy death,
That godly we may live by faith.

*A.* 9. With mouth and hand our Choir to thee
Vows homage and fidelity,
Till we our heav'nly home ſhall gain;
Thereto, Lord Jeſus, ſay Amen.

T. 235.

Till thy bride perfected ſhall be,
Cleaves heart and mind alone to thee;
O may we ſtill more clearly trace
Thy holy will and thoughts of peace;
Fulfil in us thy purpoſe all,
And in our Children great and ſmall!
Amen.

4. T.

4. T. 235.

*A.* O LORD of all confeſt,
True cauſe and fountain bleſt
Of all that bliſs and grace,
Which we, thy flock, poſſeſs:
Thou ſlaughter'd Lamb, our God and Lord,
To needy pray'rs thine ear afford;
Thy mercy on our Choir beſtow,
And to our Children favor ſhow;
For thy ſalvation, which thro' grace
We richly ſhare, accept our praiſe;
*B.* Thy love no mind can comprehend,
*S.* Thy boundleſs mercies have no end;
*A.* We humbly now 'fore thee appear
And our hearts' gratitude declare.
Amen.

T. 22. e.

1. Our motives, Lord, are numberleſs
For joy, and ſhame, and thankfulneſs;
*S.* O what is man, that we ſhould prove
Such favor'd objects of thy love?

T. 22. b.

*B.* 2. Thou waſt in human fleſh array'd,
For the whole world an off'ring made,
*S.* And thy whole life on earth for us
Was truly meritorious.

*A.* 3. Thou didſt thereby the married ſtate
*L.* (Ordain'd when thou didſt man create)
*A.* Hallow and conſecrate to be
An image of thy church and thee.

*L.* Let

*L**. Let our marriage be honorable among all men, and the bed be undefiled;

'Teach the wife to be ſubject to the huſband, as the Church is to Chriſt;

And teach the huſband to love his wife, as Chriſt loveth the Church;

But let not the creature take place to the prejudice of the Creator, or divide with Chriſt;

*A.* *Hear us, our dear Lord and God!*

T. 22. e.

4. May all thoſe bleſſings on us flow,
And in our lives their virtue ſhow,
Which from the womb unto the croſs
Thou, Lord, haſt merited for us.

*L**. Let our pregnant ſiſters reap the bleſſing of thy having lain in the womb of thy mother;

And thoſe who bring forth, of thy being brought forth into the world;

And thoſe that give ſuck, of thy having ſucked the breaſts of a mother;

Sanctify to thyſelf all fathers and mothers;

And bleſs thy gift the children!

*A.* *Hear us, our dear Lord and God!*

T. 22. d.

5. Wiſdom and faithfulneſs afford
To all the parents, gracious Lord!
Crown their endeavors with ſucceſs,
To train their children to thy praiſe.

*S.* 6. Let them be by thy Spirit led,
And thus from grace to grace proceed;
*B.* Yea, to thy Father them preſent,
Since thou for them thy life haſt ſpent.

* This prayer is read.

T. 235.

*A.* To husbands, wives, and children, Lord,
All needful grace and gifts afford;
Grant us to yield thee joy, since we
Are thy redeemed property,
And in each family thy will
And all thy purposes fulfil.
Amen.

V.

# LITANIES OF THE WIDOWERS.

1. T. 235.

*A.* O HOLY Father, God,
Of the Lord of Sabaoth!
Abba, O God, our God,
Thro' our Lord's death and blood!
The Cherubim and Seraphs cloud
Exalt thy praiſe with voices loud;
*L.* The Elders worſhipping fall down
And caſt their crowns before thy throne;
*A.* With them we alſo proſtrate fall,
And thee Jehovah Abba call.
Amen.

T. 22. b.

*L.* 1. Like Simeon we with heart and voice
In God our Savior will rejoice;
May our thank-off'rings always be,
Dear Father, pleaſing unto thee!

*A.* 2. Us all in mercy own and bleſs
As members of thy choſen race,
By Chriſt preſented unto thee,
As his reward and property.

3. O may we, thro' thy grace, while here,
In Chriſt's ſalvation have our ſhare;

In him accept us graciously,
And lead us till his face we see.

T. 22. a.

4. O Holy Ghost, make thine abode
In us, as temples of our God,
That we, 'midst Jesu's flock of grace,
In all things, may show forth his praise.

5. And let thy peace upon us rest,
Thy goodness may we ever taste;
Let us in our sabbatic state
The joys of Heav'n anticipate.

T. 22. l.

6. Jesus, Redeemer of mankind,
*L.* In whom alone we comfort find;
*A.* Let spirit, soul, and body share
Thy merits and thy tender care.

7. Fill us with peace, and joy, and love,
*L.* And our support in trials prove;
When weaknesses of age appear,
Keep thou our minds and senses clear.

8. This be our aim on earth, thy will
To seek in all things to fulfil,
And when thou call'st, prepar'd to be
To leave this world and go to thee.

T. 235.

*L.* When all our toil is o'er, how blest
Will be our lot, with thee to rest;
*A.* What joys divine shall we then feel,
What pleasures, which no tongue can tell,
When we in perfect happiness
Shall once behold thee face to face!
Amen.

2. T. 235.

*A.* FATHER of Chriſt our Lord,
A gracious ear afford,
*L.* When with imperfect lays
The wid'wers give thee praiſe:
*A.* For having from eternity
Elected us, through mercy free,
In Chriſt to endleſs happineſs,
Which this life's troubles far out-weighs:
O turn to us thy countenance,
Amidſt our wants and indigence.
Amen.

T. 22. b.

1. Thanks for thy kind paternal love,
Which we in Chriſt ſo richly prove,
That we our truſt upon thy grace
With filial confidence can place;

2. That thou for Jeſu's ſake wilt bleſs
Our Choir unto the end of days,
Since we're in him belov'd by thee,
And ſhare his gifts abundantly,

*L.* 3. As children by the Comforter
Taught, to cry Abba without fear,
And who are clothed in the dreſs
Of thy Son's blood-bought righteouſneſs.

T. 22. a.

*A.* 4. Give us new tokens, Lord, we pray,
Of thy great goodneſs ev'ry day,
With thy paternal faithfulneſs
And boundleſs mercy us embrace.

5. Thy joyful Spirit, which doth cry,
Abba, and Jesus glorify,
Teach us, while here on earth we are,
To spend our time in praise and pray'r:

6. When we go to the sanctuary,
For us and for the Church to pray,
Grant our requests for Jesu's sake,
And let us of thy grace partake.

T. 22. l.

7. Jesus, thou slaughter'd Lamb of God,
Who didst assume our flesh and blood,
*L.* And by thy blood, for sinners shed,
Hast for the world a ransom paid;

*A.* 8. Present us to thy Father, Lord,
As thy own purchase and reward,
That he may own us graciously,
And over us rejoice in thee.

9. O lead us daily by the hand,
Till we shall reach the promis'd land,
Let us in need be ne'er depriv'd
Of comforts from thy death deriv'd.

T. 235.

Thus shall we, fill'd with joy and peace,
Proceed t' enjoy that happiness,
Which here to us is freely giv'n,
And which the ransom'd hosts in Heav'n,
Who worshipping 'fore thee appear,
For ever in thy presence share.
Amen.

3. T. 235.

*A.* THEE, holy triune God!
We magnify and laud;
Accept the worſhip, thanks, and praiſe
Of us, thy wid'wers, for the grace,
Which thou ſo richly haſt diſplay'd
To us in Chriſt, our Lord and Head!
Amen.

T. 22. b.

1. O Father, thee we thank and praiſe,
Who pitiedſt us, a fallen race,
And gav'ſt thy dear and only Son,
For us loſt ſinners to atone.

*L.* 2. Remember now his wounds and croſs,
And be a father unto us;
*A.* Crown us with mercies; let us be
In him well pleaſing unto thee.

T. 22. o.

3. God Holy Ghoſt, bleſt Comforter,
With grateful hearts we thee revere,
For having taught us to believe
In Chriſt, and by this faith to live.

4. Preſerve us henceforth in his grace,
Teach us more fully yet to trace
The counſel of his love, and keep
Us all with him in fellowſhip.

T. 22. l.

*L.* 5. O how divine thy comforts are,
Lord Jeſus! what delicious fare

Is

Is this, when we thy presence feel,
And thou thy kindness dost reveal.

A. 6. We render thee our thanks and praise,
That thou, in these our mortal days,
Such grace and love on us bestow'st,
And worship thee, bow'd in the dust.

T. 22. d.

7. Help us, thy servants, gracious God,
L. Who are redeemed with thy blood,
A. And grant us, for thy suff'rings sake,
Of thy salvation to partake.

8. We thee entreat to set us free,
Lord, from whate'er displeases thee,
O may our walk be to thy praise,
And to the glory of thy grace:

T. 235.

Until, when all our trials cease,
Our hopes of future joy and bliss
Are realiz'd, and we, thro' grace,
Are call'd to see thee face to face;
O welcome day! at thy return,
Lord Jesus, we shall cease to mourn.
Amen.

4. T. 235.

A. LORD Jesus, Prince of peace,
Thou only source of grace
And true felicity,
Now and eternally:
The blessings on our Choir bestow,
Which from thy holy merits flow,

And draw unto our hearts so near,
As if we saw thee present here:
Thus we celestial joys shall taste,
Till called hence with thee to rest.
Amen.

T. 22. a.

1. Thy poverty and weakliness
*L.* In servant's form and lowliness,
*A.* Make us contented with our own,
While in this vale of tears we groan.

*L.* 2. Thy watching, fasting, and the pray'rs,
Thou offer'dst with strong cries and tears,
*A.* That deep distress, which night and day
For us, so heavy on thee lay,

*L.* 3. Yea, all thy suff'rings, Lamb of God,
*A.* Atoning death and precious blood,
*L.* Whereby thou life for us didst gain,
*A.* Our comfort, joy, and strength remain.

T. 22. b.

4. Thy resting in the silent tomb,
Thy rising, having death o'ercome,
And then ascending gloriously,
To sit upon thy throne on high,

5. Thy coming to thy Church again,
Or our release from sin and pain,
By being called home to thee,
Comfort us, Lord, abundantly.

T. 22. d.

*L.* 6. The wid'wers chief concern while here,
Is, for thy coming to prepare,

Thy

Thy consolation to await,
Like Simeon ready thee to meet.

*A.* 7. Then at the end of all distress
We shall depart to thee in peace,
And shall behold thy face most bright
In joy and everlasting light.

T. 22. o.

*L.* 8. But if it be thy holy will,
That we, tho' weary, serve thee still,
Grant us, thy name to glorify,
To thee to live, to thee to die.

T. 235.

*A.* O grant, that till our lips grow cold,
We may in spirit thee behold,
As thou upon th' accursed cross
Didst shed thy blood and die for us,
And that we with our latest breath
May praise thee for thy wounds and death.
Amen.

# VI.

## LITANIES OF THE WIDOWS.

### I*. T. 235.

*A.* MOST holy Trinity,
We praiſe and honor thee,
That by the counſel of thy grace
We're fore-ordain'd to happineſs,
Thro' Jeſus Chriſt, the Son of God,
Who in our place as ſurety ſtood,
Became a man, and death ſuſtain'd,
And thereby our ſalvation gain'd.
O might each pulſe thankſgiving beat,
And ev'ry breath his praiſe repeat!
Amen.

T. 22. b.

*L.* 1. This wonder makes our hearts to glow,
And cauſes grateful tears to flow,
That God himſelf became a man,
And was for our redemption ſlain.

*A.* 2. Moſt holy bleſſed Trinity,
We praiſe thee to eternity;
O may the widows choir partake
Of choiceſt bleſſings for Chriſt's ſake.

T. 22. a.

3. Thou who as children us doſt own
*L.* Thro' Jeſus thy beloved Son,

* *A.* is ſung by the Widows, *L.* by the Liturgiſt.

G *A.* And

*A.* And whom we by the Holy Ghoſt
Call Abba, Father, with full truſt,

4. Thro' Jeſus Chriſt, now bleſs our Choir,
With all we want, or can deſire,
Preſerve us in his love, and be
Our gracious God eternally.

T. 22. o.

*L.* 5. Lord Jeſus Chriſt, our higheſt good,
Who haſt redeem'd us by thy blood,
And purchas'd for us life and grace,
*A.* Be thou our comfort in diſtreſs.

6. O may our ſouls and bodies be
Devoted wholly unto thee;
*L.* However weak we are, our aim
Shall be to glorify thy name.

*A.* 7. The comforts of the Holy Ghoſt
Grant us: Our weakneſſes thou know'ſt;
And while we keep our ſabbath here,
For endleſs glory us prepare.

T. 22. d.

8. God Holy Ghoſt, give us the grace,
To ſhow our cordial thankfulneſs,
*L.* And let our needy ſouls by faith
Feed on the merits of Chriſt's death.

*A.* May we, like Anna, perſevere
By day and night in conſtant pray'r, (Luke, ii. 36.)
And daily taught and led by thee,
True happy widows learn to be,

10. Whoſe converſation is above
With Chriſt, whom, tho' unſeen, they love,
And for his coming humbly wait,
In joyful hope, the Lord to meet.

T. 235.

O may this be our only care,
While we as pilgrims ſojourn here,
That we may yield delight to him,
Rejoicing in that bleſſed time,
When Chriſt our Savior ſhall appear,
And wipe away our ev'ry tear:
Then ſin and ſorrow will be fled,
And everlaſting joys ſucceed.
Amen.

21 T. 235.

*A.* O LORD, the widows friend,
Whoſe thoughts of peace extend
Beyond what words can e'er expreſs,
Surpaſſing all our thanks and praiſe;
*L.* What love can be compar'd with thine,
Who didſt for us thy life reſign!
*A.* Moſt gracious Savior, we fall down
And humbly worſhip at thy throne.
Amen.

T. 22. b.

1. Thanks for thy birth, incarnate God,
Thanks for thy ſuff'rings, death, and blood,
The ſource of our felicity,
In time and in eternity.

*L.* 2. All thoſe who cleave to thee by faith,
Have part in thy atoning death,
Whereby they're bleſt already here,
And ſhall in Heav'n thy glory ſhare.

T. 22. a.

*A.* 3. This we experience, and rejoice,
Lord Jeſus, in thy ſacrifice,
Which richly hath reſtored all
What we had loſt thro' Adam's fall.

*L.* 4. Might we acknowledge and improve
The bleſſings of redeeming love,
Which have been merited by thee
For time and for eternity!

T. 22. e.

*A.* 5. May on our hearts thy bitter pain
Indelibly impreſs'd remain,
And grant, that for thy ſoul's diſtreſs,
We all may magnify thy grace.

6. Lord, let us in this world of ſtrife
Draw comfort from thy ſuff'ring life;
This be our balm for each complaint,
Our ſtrength, when mind or body faint,

T. 22. d.

7. Till we, who here muſt often weep,
In Heav'n eternal joys ſhall reap;
Where thou'ſt prepar'd for us a place,
And we ſhall ſee thee face to face.

T. 22. f.

*L.* 8. To Chriſt, dear widows, cloſely cleave,
And in communion with him live,
Till he ſhall ſay to you: "Ye bleſt,
"Enter into my joy and reſt."

T. 235.

*A.* What joy, what happineſs complete,
Doth us poor needy ſheep await,

When

When after light afflictions we
Shall to the Shepherd gather'd be,
Who graciously will in that day
Wipe from our eyes all tears away.
Amen.

3. T. 235.

A. FATHER of Christ, the Word,
The Father, God and Lord
Of Jesu's flock, since he
Our brother deign'd to be:

T. 22. b.

1. Thou gav'st thy only Son for us,
From whom life everlasting flows,
And since we now thy children are,
Tho' poor, we're objects of thy care.

L. 2. Think on his death, impart thy aid
To us, in ev'ry time of need,
And let us constantly, while here,
In his salvation have a share.

A. 3. Thy mercy, Lord, to us dispense,
According to our confidence;
Grant in our lonely state, that we
With Jesus may one spirit be.

T. 235.

Jesus, our Lord and God,
Who took'st our flesh and blood,
And to deliver us,
Diedst on th' accursed cross.

T. 22. o.

4. Since thou thy blood for us hast shed,
Thou art our comfort in all need,

And

And turn'st thy all-reviving face
Unto our poverty in grace.

5. Thy mercy is an endless store,
Each day displays to us still more
Thy tender love and faithfulness,
Beyond whate'er our thanks express.

6. Thou list'nest to the widows' pray'rs,
And countest all their sighs and tears;
Each sorrow, whether small or great,
Thy comforts can alleviate.

T. 235.

*A.* God Holy Ghost, to thee,
Praises for ever be,
Who dost, as Comforter,
To us Christ's love declare,

T. 22. f.

7. That each church member's made to be
A living temple unto thee,
That thou dost comfort them in time,
And once wilt lead them home to him.

*L.* 8. In thee each widow may confide,
As in her guardian, friend and guide,
Since Jesus Christ, with this intent,
Thee from the Father to us sent.

*A.* 9. Our hearts we open unto thee;
O dwell in us continually,
And fill our souls with joy and peace,
Spirit of glory and of grace!

T. 235.

Most holy blessed Trinity!
We praise thee to eternity,
And honor thee, through Jesus Christ,
Our Mediator and High Priest,

Who

Who gloriously fulfill'd the plan
Thou formedst to redeem lost man.
Amen.

4. T. 235.

*A.* JESUS, thy praise we sing,
To thee our thanks we bring,
That thou thy glory didst forsake,
Of all our sorrows to partake;
*L.* O love unutterably great,
Thy suff'rings cancel all our debt,
And by thy all-atoning blood,
We're made acceptable to God;
*A.* What are our thanks? With deepest shame
We prostrate, and adore thy name.
Amen.

T. 22. b.

*L.* 1. Should not the widows choir rejoice,
And praise thee, Lord, with heart and voice?
*A.* Yea, thee we gratefully confess
The source of all our happiness.

2. Since thou this greatest grace hast shown,
By death for all our sins t' atone,
The smallest thou wilt surely grant,
And well supply our ev'ry want.

T. 22. c.

*L.* 3. God will the widows ne'er forsake.
*A.* To Him we may our refuge take,
And on his care and faithfulness,
All our dependance firmly place.

4. A widow, who her son belov'd
With tears bemoan'd, his pity mov'd; (Luke, vii. 31.)
His mother he did recommend,
When on the cross, to John his friend.

*L.* 5. You're likewiſe objects of his care,
Since Scripture plainly doth declare,
That to the church this charge he gave:
Widows to honor and relieve.

T. 22. a.

*A.* 6. For this our gracious Lord we praiſe,
May we be faithful thro' his grace,
And walking humbly in his ſight,
In all we do, yield him delight.

*L.* 7. To love the Lord, be your firſt care,
The next, to ſerve his people here;
*A.* Can we do good, we'll it embrace,
He'll us reward with looks of grace.

8. When in each other's walk and mien
True peace and happineſs is ſeen:
This mutual pleaſure does afford,
And cauſes us to thank our Lord.

9. O when the ſlaughter'd Lamb appears,
We can't with-hold our grateful tears,
Th' impreſſion of his bitter death
Preſerves and does increaſe our faith.

T. 22. d.

*L.* 10. This be engraven in your breaſt,
Long as this dying life ſhall laſt,
And may your Savior in this time
Unite you cloſely unto him.

T. 235.

*A.* O draw us nearer to thee ſtill,
Grant us, we humbly pray, to feel
Thy preſence both by night and day,
Whether we work, or reſt, or pray,
And may at thy appearing we,
Lord Jeſus Chriſt, be found in thee!
Amen.

www.ingramcontent.com/pod-product-compliance
Lightning Source LLC
Chambersburg PA
CBHW031447270326
41930CB00007B/898